# NIGHT LIGHTS & PILLOW FIGHTS

## T W O

# NIGHT & LIGHTS
# PILLOW & FIGHTS
## T W O

# THE BOX SET

POEMS AND PICTURES BY

*Guy Gilchrist*

**PUBLISHING**

Canton, CT

JOIN GUY GILCHRIST'S
STORY LAND CLUB
Quarterly - Classic Stories -
Comics - News - & Fun

Gilchrist Publishing
P.O. Box 1194
Canton, CT 06019

**Night Lights & Pillow Fights II:  The Box Set**

GILCHRIST PUBLISHING EDITION
Copyright © 1997 by Guy Gilchrist
World rights reserved.
Gilchrist Publishing • P.O. Box 1194 • Canton, CT 06019
http://www.gilchriststudios.com

GILCHRIST PUBLISHING

Printed in the United States of America
First Gilchrist Publishing Printing: October 1997

This book is dedicated
with love
to the light and the joy in my life. . .
my wife, Angie.
Thanks, Darlin'.

# ACKNOWLEDGMENTS

First, I'd like to thank my wife, my brother, my kids and anybody that's come into the studio over the last seven or eight years, looked in the old files, and said, "Guy, you oughtta make a book out of those poems in that box. . . before you lose' em." You were right, so I did. But, before all those loose papers could become a book, they had to be gathered, edited, and scanned. First, as a weekly feature for my local hometown paper.

To Brad, who worked on it first, thanks. And. . .

To Jed and Alan at *The Voice* newspapers, for running my column, and your support and enthusiasm for this project, thank you.

To Nicki Brewer, for all your hard work turning these piles of typing paper and Bristol Board into something. And Carolyn Morgan, for your super contributions to the layout and mechanicals. Thanks, Ladies! Now, we've got a book!

I'd also like to thank all the people that read my poems in the paper, and my other books, and share with me how much they enjoy what I do, and how my work has touched their lives. I want you all to know that *your* stories have touched *my* life. You are the reason I do what I do.

And finally my thanks to God, for allowing me to do what I love to do for a living. I am truly blessed, and the Glory, God, is yours.

# BEARSKIN HUG

I do not want
A bearskin rug.
I'd rather have
A bearskin hug.

# MARVIN THE MONSTER

Marvin the Monster's all tucked in his bed,
But Marvin the Monster's not sleeping.
Marvin the Monster's so frightfully scared
Of the nightmare he thinks that is creeping.
What is this terrible nightmare?
This scary thought stuck in his head?
Marvin the Monster's afraid of the... YOU!
That is hiding right under his bed!

# BIG FISH

How big is that fish at the end of my line?
Is it 7 feet long?  Maybe 8?  Maybe 9?
It must be 10 feet long with a mouth twice as wide,
With a tail big as Texas!  Big fins on the side!
That's a mighty big fish.  That's all I've got to say.
That's a mighty big fish...
    That
      just
        got
          away . . .

# THE BIG
# FAT MOON AND
# THE SHOOTING STAR

"Do you know where you are going?
Do you know just how far?"
Said the Big Fat Moon to the Shooting Star.
Said the Shooting Star to the Big Fat Moon
"I do know how far . . . but I don't know how soon.
I don't know how long I will be around
My life goes by so fast
And I burn myself up as I shoot through the sky
So I know that I can't last."
"Then go slower," said the Moon to the Shooting Star
"Do as I do and hang in the sky
Don't burn so fast or quite so bright.
Take it easy, or surely you'll die."
But the Shooting Star just blazed on and on
Till he disappeared into the blue.
But not before he was wished upon
And a few of those wishes came true.

# WE'RE THE GANG

We're the gang of big fat squirrels.
We don't like birds.
We don't like girls.
We don't like dogs.
We don't like mice.
And we live on your porch
so you better be nice.
You better bring us your bird seed,
at least twice a day.
Just drop it outside,
then just go on your way.
We know you think you got the seed
to feed those stupid things.
Those things in the trees
with the feathers and the wings.
But first we've got to get our share.
Then we'll leave some for them
if we have some to spare.
But we don't like birds, or dogs, or girls.
'Cause we're the gang of big fat squirrels.

# A TROLL NAMED MCMEARD

There once was a troll named McMeard,
Who carried his stuff in his beard.
He could travel to places,
Without his suitcases.
Pretty smart for a troll, but still weird.

# POOR MILDRED MUTTON

Did you hear about Poor Mildred Mutton?
Alas, she had no belly button.
So, with a needle and thread,
She sewed on a zipper instead.
Hey!  A zipper is better than nuttin'!

# THE BATTLE OF
# THE BATHTUB

Swashbuckler Rosie
　Sunk Pirate Joe's sub
　　With a swash and a buckle
　　Last night in the tub.
With a buck and a swashle
　A swashle and a buck.
　　So Pirate Joe sank
　　Rosie's best rubber duck.

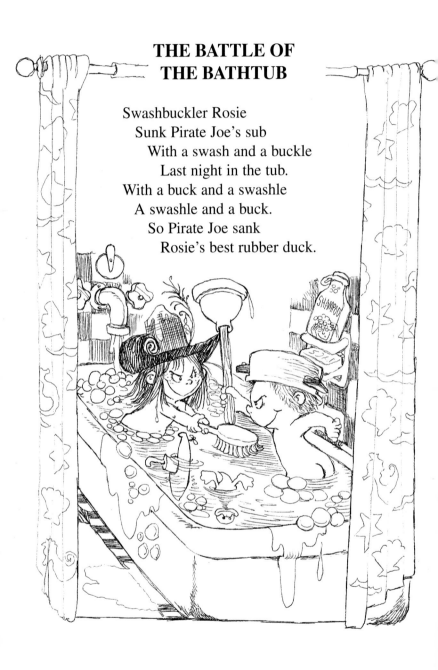

## CYNTHIA SARAH LAROFF

"I don't want to think!
   I don't want to think!"
      Said Cynthia Sarah LaRoff.
"I don't want to think!
   It's way too much work!"
      BOOM!  Cindy's head fell off.

# THE BEST EXCUSE NOTE
# MORT EVER
# WROTE HIMSELF

Dear Teacher,
Please excuse my dear son, Mort
For forgetting to do his book report.
It's not like him you know,
He's extremely bright.
But he has an excuse.
Here's what happened last night. . .
There was sweet Mort,
Fast asleep in his bed ---
When a werewolf came in
And he unscrewed his head.
He reached in Mort's head
And he took out his brain,
Then he tossed it in the sink
And it went down the drain.
Then in place of his brain,
He poured cobwebs and dust,
Some scrambled eggs too,
And some graham cracker crust.
Then the werewolf just vanished
Right into the blue. . .
Could you do your homework
If THIS happened to you?
And since Mort has no brain,
Until we find another. . .
Don't make him do homework.
Sincerely,

My Mother

# MATH MADE EASY

Learning math is no big fuss.
Just ask your hippopotamus.
There's no one better at minus and pluses
Than a real smart hippopotamus is.
But. . .
If you don't have a hippo to help you out,
Don't throw your notebook, and
Don't scream and pout!
Don't wish for the Hippo that you never had,
Don't have a breakdown, and go ask your Dad!
'Cause you know that your daddy is no wiz at math.
So, if you don't have a hippo, go ask your Girathe.

# BIG FOOTED GEORGE

While hiking around the Oregon Gorge
I met a big creature called Big-footed George.
He showed me around on the Oregon Trail,
While I hung on tightly to his hairy tail.
He showed me the river, he showed me Mount Hood.
As a tour guide, I tell ya, Big George was real good.
Now I knew no one would believe I had met Big-footed George.
So when George finished showing me around the whole gorge,
I asked if I could take a picture, and George said, "You bet."
So I reached in my knapsack, my camera to get.
But I ran out of film, so I didn't get the shot.
Then George said, "Sorry" and I said, "Thanks a lot."
Now if you don't believe me, if you think that I lie...
Go meet him yourself, and tell George I said "Hi!"

# TANGLED UP ON THE MOON

I got tangled up on the moon last night.
My hair got caught on a crater.
I always say, "I'll get it cut"
But I always put it off until later.
So it shouldn't come as a shock to me,
that last night as I flew
I got tangled up on the moon last night...
Has this ever happened to you?

# A PIG ON BROADWAY

Once upon a time,
I think the time was five-thirty,
Lived a pig in a pen,
All muddy and dirty.
Peter the pig lived there
With his mammy and pappy
In the mud of the pigpen.
But Pete wasn't happy.
"What's the trouble?" asked Mammy,
"Pete, you seem awfully blue
Doesn't mud make you happy?
Pete? What's wrong with you?"
"No offense," said young Peter,
"But I don't *like* this mud.
I don't like the *slop*
And the *dirt* and the *crud*!
I want to live in a penthouse!
In New York!" shouted Peter.
"I want to be famous! A star of the theatre!"
For you and dear Daddy, this life is okay
But, Mom, I was born for the stage of Broadway!"

So he packed up his suitcase with corn on the cob
And he set off for Broadway in search of a job.
First, he took lessons in singing and dance.
Then he begged the producers to give him a chance.
He tried singing opera and dancing ballet ...
"We can't use a pig," the Directors would say.
He tried tap dancing, waltzes and dancing the jig ...
"Sorry kid," said the producers ... "We can't use a pig."
And just when it looked like the end for poor Peter. . .
He saw an ad for a job at the Will Shakespeare Theatre.
So he read his audition with all of his heart,
And he read it so well that they gave Pete the part.
Then, Pete was so proud that he called Arkansas!
And sent front row tickets to dear Paw and Maw
And they came to New York to the Big Broadway show!
And when Pete walked on stage, they were in the front row!
And the show was a hit that was bigger than big!!
"Hamlet" a play starring Peter the Pig.

## WHAT IS IT?

Deeper than the ocean.
  Sudden as a breeze.
Always there
  Like clouds and air,
    Growing like the trees.
Cozy warm like sweaters.
  Fuzzier than socks.
Sweet like maple syrup.
  Older than the rocks.
Brighter than a birthday.
  Longer than a mile.
Bigger than the universe.
  Lighter than a smile.
Sparkly like soda pop
  That tickles when it fizzes.
Someone thinking of you
  Love's the thing that this is.

# A PORCUPINE AND A BUNNY IN LOVE

Kiss me a kiss
Full of passion and thrills!
OUCH!!  OUCH!!  OUCH!!
OUCH!!  OUCH!!  OUCH!!
Sorry honey, pardon my quills.

# THE PURPLE PREENING PRUNING PRORD

The Purple Preening Pruning Prord
Likes to ride in my V-8 Ford
And to make doubly sure that we never get bored
He plays Beatles songs on his whos-a-ma-gourd.

## MY DOG

I wonder what my dog does
When I leave her alone.
Does she lie on the rug
With her small rawhide bone?
Does she wait for me quietly,
There on the rug,
Till I come through the front door
And give her a hug?
Or does she throw away her old bone, and
Order some pizza, by dialing the phone?
Then call all her dog friends:
The girls and boys?
Then play all my records
And dance to the noise?
Maybe she and her doggie friends
Dress in my clothes,
Then go turn on the TV and
Go watch doggie shows?
Then she puts on my apron,
My chef's hat and shoes,
And thaws out some steaks
For some swell barbeques?
Do they go through my pockets,
In my best overalls?
Pull out my wallet
And go to the malls?

And buy lots of doggie toys,
Biscuits and balls
With my credit cards
Taken from my overalls?
Then do they rush back and
Clean up at the end of the day?
Does she make sure her doggie friends
All go away . . .
So she can pose sweetly
On the rug on the floor?
So she looks like she's sleeping
When I come through the door?
Maybe I'm crazy . . .
And maybe I'm not.
You see, I just got my credit card bill . . .
And I owe a lot.

# MY BASEBALL
# CARDS

I keep all my baseball cards under my bed:
Every Giant and Yankee and Padre and Red,
Every Cub, every Brewer and Boston Red Sox.
I keep 'em all here in their own little box.
The Tigers, The Mariners, all of the 'Jays,
The Dodgers, the Angels and all of the A's.
The Pirates and Phillies and lest I forget,
Every White Sox and Cardinal, and every Met.

I keep all my cards in a box that says, "Shoes."
And I keep 'em in order so I never lose
Any Indians, Rangers, or any Expos,
Or Astros, or Royals, or Baltimore O's.
And I read all the backs, all the hits, runs, and saves
Of all of my Twins and my Atlanta Braves.
I've got every baseball card they made.
Except for ONE GUY that you have . . .
WANNA TRADE ? ? ?

# THE
# WISHAMOO

The Wishamoo
Says, "I love you,"
Over and over and over.
And over and over
And over and over
And over and over AND OVER.
The Wishamoo
Says, "I love you,"
Like it's going to say it forever.
The Wishamoo
Says, "I love you."
Will it ever stop saying it ever?
The Wishamoo
Says, "I love you,"
And it's really, really starting to bug me.
I just wish for once,
It would shut its yap! . . .
And . . .
Come over
  Here and
    Hug me.

# RAMONA'S
# MAGIC RADIO

Ramona bought a radio made of wood and tubes and wires.
She bought it at a tag sale.  It was sitting on some tires.
Ramona didn't even know if it worked.
It was, after all, quite old.
But she liked it's shape, the cherrywood, the dials . . .
She was sold.
So Ramona took her treasure home
And plugged it in the wall.
From behind the glass came a golden flash
That was warm and bright and small.
It flickered off. . .  and on. . .  and off. . .
Then it finally lit up the numbers,
Like an old man fast asleep too long,
Just awaking from his slumbers.
Then the dial light began to glow a long and steady glow . . .
And from the burlap speakers came a song from long ago.
A song not heard for years.  A gentle, sentimental song.
A breezy, easy melody played on and on and on.
Ramona hummed along a bit.
Ramona danced a while.
Then she reached out for the tuning knob
And slowly turned the dial.
But, no matter where she turned it to, the radio wouldn't play
Any other kinds of songs, but songs from yesterday.
No.  The radio only played the past.
No modern melodies.
It's as if the radio wanted to tell someone
It's favorite memories.
So, Ramona dances to her radio
Playing songs from way-back-when.
I guess Ramona needed the radio . . .
And the radio needed a friend.

# HUCKLEBERRY DOUGHNUT'S AMAZING TECHNICOLOR NOSE

Huckleberry Doughnut goes a boppin' down the streets,
Lookin' like a rainbow to the people that he meets.
Lookin' like a rainbow, good ol' Huckleberry goes. . .
Huckleberry Doughnut and his technicolor nose.
His nose lights up in colors!  There for everyone to see!
Amazing, different colors like your favorite Christmas tree.
See, Huckleberry Doughnut's mouth
Can't speak one single word
But the colors of his nose say things so very rarely heard.
If you ask Huck how today will be
And Huck's nose turns cherry red ---
You know that Huckleberry sees a rosy day ahead.
And if his nose turns orange, like an orange in a crate ---
That means there's no telling what great thing
Today you might create.
You might create a painting that is full of life and bright. . .
Or a song, or dance, or a friendship or two,
'Cause Huck's nose says "you might!"
If you ask Huck "How you feelin', Huck?"
And his nose turns sunny yellow ---
Huckleberry Doughnut feels all warm, and light, and mellow.
You know his heart is full of love if his nose turns kelly green,
Or emeraldish, or grassy pine, or some green in between.
If you tell old Huck your favorite dream
And his nose turns a purplish hue ---
That means if you believe in it,
Your dream will surely come true.
Yeah. . .  Huckleberry Doughnut's
Pretty special, I suppose.
It's not every day you meet someone
With a rainbow up his nose!

# THE CAT
# I'VE GOT

The cat I've got is really shy.
That's how she is.  I don't know why.
She hides under towels on the very top shelf
Of the bathroom closet, all by herself.
And she won't come out when friends stop by.
The cat I've got is really shy.
But when we're alone, then she doesn't hide.
She jumps on my bed, and she sleeps at my side.
She nuzzles and cuddles, and huggles and purrs,
With that special cat motor sound of hers.
But when the morning comes around,
She sneaks away without a sound.
She goes under the towels in the closet up high.
The cat I've got is really shy.

# LITTLE BEAU JAMES

Little Beau James was as tall as my knees,
As I stood there in line with my ten groceries.
Little Beau James stood in line with his Dad.
They were in front of me with the groceries they had.
We were bored. We were waiting, not saying a thing. . .
Then Little Beau James . . . he decided to sing.
He sang up a storm full of songs with no names!
His father said, "Not in the grocery store, James.
Please James, don't sing, just wait here quietly!
Please! Not so loud! They're all looking at me!
I'm getting embarrassed!" said the Dad in the store.
But James didn't stop. He just sang more and more.
Then finally they got to the head of the line.
His dad bought his stuff while I unloaded mine.
Then his Dad grabbed his groceries and pulled James along.
Goodbye Little Beau James . . . and thanks for the song.

# THE MATTRESS MUNCHING SCHMED

Beware!  You monkeys that jump on the bed.
  Beware of the
    Mattress
      Munching
      Schmed.
Just when you think that nobody is looking,
  And you get bouncing good and you really get cooking. . .
When you get that BOING BOING going in both your legs,
  And your brain gets to bouncing like scrambly eggs,
When you're suspended high above your bed . . .
  There comes the
    Mattress
      Munching
      Schmed!
He'll gobble your bed in a half second flat!
  Then he'll leave with a grin, and a tip of his hat.
By the time you come down from your place in the air . . .
  The Schmed will be gone and your bed won't be there.
But, you know,
  For a monster . . .
He's not a bad fellow.
  The Schmed eats your bed . . .
But he leaves you your
          PILLOW.

# I'M AN OLD COWHAND

I'm an old cowhand
At the hot dog stand.
I've got a cap gun so reach for the skies!
I've got a cap gun, hand over the fries!
Give me a cheeseburger!
No!  Make it a double!
I'm an old cowhand . . .
Just looking for trouble.

# A CHRISTMAS DEAL

I'll tell you how the reindeer fly
If you let me borrow a dime.
For a quarter I'll tell you how
Santa Claus fits down your chimney every time.
For a dollar I'll tell you where he lives,
And I'll draw you a map so you'll find it.
And I'll tell you about his toy shop and
How he parks his sled behind it.
I really need the money!
And I know this stuff! I do!
I need a dollar and thirty-five cents
So I can buy something for you!

# HOPPY,
# THE RANGER,
# AND ROY

Hoppy, The Ranger, and Roy.
The heroes of this little boy.
A silver bullet
A "You're welcome, ma'am."
They're all part of what I am.
Hoppy, The Ranger, and Roy.
A treasure chest full of their toys.
With my hat tilted right,
A cap pistol that gleamed,
And a head full of big western dreams.
Sage brush and canyons and rustlers,
Shifty bandits and river boat hustlers.
No need to worry, all wrongs are set right
In glorious, full black and white.
They never accepted any pay.
They'd just smile and gallop away . . .
Leave the bad guys in tears and the townfolk in joy,
Hoppy, The Ranger, and Roy.

# GERALD JOE HAROLD MCSNUFF

My name is
   Gerald Joe Harold M$^c$Snuff.
I will now attempt
   To do everyday stuff.
Give me a drum roll,
   If you please . . .
I will now attempt
   To touch my knees.
Give me a brassy
   Rat-a-tat-tat!
I will now attempt
   To feed my cat.
Give me a spotlight
   Of silver-white-blue!
I will now attempt
   To tie my shoe.
Play me a tribute
   By 12 trumpeteers!
I'm about to attempt . . .
   Washing behind my own ears.
My name is
   Gerald Joe Harold M$^c$Snuff.
I get standing ovations
   For doing everyday stuff.

# HAVE YOU MET HER MAJESTY?

Have you met her majesty?
Her sloppy highness Rose Marie?
Who sits on a trash heap 10 feet tall
Of dirty socks, and overalls,
And wadded up paper, and paperback books,
And tennis balls, and picture hooks,
and sneakers, sacks, and magazines,
and jingle bells, and jellybeans.
I've met her and I like her fine.
Her trash heap looks a lot like mine!

## FEAR

Here he comes. Here comes FEAR.
How'd that monster get in here?
He must have tunneled through my floor . . .
Or oozed in underneath my door.
I thought I'd not see him again . . .
But here comes FEAR, nobody's friend.
Here comes his pals, the I DON'T KNOWS.
They're nipping, snipping at my toes!
Closer they come!
So I face them and say,
"I ain't scared of you guys!"
And they all run away.

# DANCIN' CROWS

Dancin' crows in dancin' clothes
Do mambo-bops & doe-see-does
And whirly-wops & go-go-goes!
Those dancin' crows got twinkle-toes.

# SUMMERTIME, SUMMERTIME SONG

Summertime, summertime
Popping bubblegummer time
Summertime, summertime song.
Summertime, summertime
Lay around and bummertime
Summertime, summertime song.
Lying in a hammock
Sleeping 'tween the treez.
Snoozing in the sunshine
Floating like a breeze.
Summertime, summertime
Hotter than a hummertime
Summertime, summertime song.
Twittling your toezees,
Glass of lemonade.
Sunburn on your nozie
Better find the shade.
Summertime, summertime
Popping bubblegummer time
Lay around and bummertime
Hotter than a hummertime
Couldn't be a funnertime
Summertime, summertime song!

# FRED AND ZELDA

"It must get awfully drafty," said Zelda to Fred.
"Walking around with a wide open head."
You see Fred's head was open.  The top wasn't there.
Right above his eyebrows where there ought to be hair.
"My head might be draftier than yours," Fred supposed.
"It might be a might tighter, if my head was closed.
But I like it like this, Zelda, that I must say.
It catches so many things that fall down my way.
Now, some things it catches can be a real pain. . .

Like snowflakes, and walnuts, and baseballs and rain.
But I clean all those out when they happen to drop
Down into this head I've got open on top.
I clean it out waiting for dreams to come by
And ideas, thoughts, and wisdom that fall from the sky.
And some day when my head's full of good things like that
When I'm full up with good stuff,
Then I might wear a hat.
But until then I'll stay open headed," Fred said.
"It must get awfully drafty," said Zelda to Fred.

# I WANT . . .

I want silver.  I want gold.
I want fame and wealth untold.
I want you.  I want friends.
I want love, and hugs, and happiness!
And fun that never ends.
I got it!  Hey!  I got it all!
I got everything!  I had a ball!
I got a punch of pleasures
Flowing from a shining cup!
I got it, got it, GOT IT ALL!
And then . . .
                    Well, . . .
                              I woke up.

## I DIDN'T KNOW

I didn't know I had a question
    Till the answer fell out of the sky.
I didn't know that I was lonely
    Till a friend came riding by.
I didn't know how good today would be
    Till the Sun had gone to bed.
Maybe the key to being happy
    Is to keep an empty head.

# LET'S TRADE

Let's trade clothes,
And see how it goes.
Let's change faces.
Let's change places.
Let's change brains, and bodies, and heads,
So we can be each other instead.
You can be me,
And I can be you.
Let's trade for just a day or two.
I'll fool your father!
You'll fool my mother!
And maybe we'll understand each other.

## THERE'S A HOLE IN THE SKY

There's a hole in the sky where the rays come through.
And nobody seems to know just what to do.
They don't know what to do, or don't know how to try
To start fixing up that big hole in the sky.
I guess you can't plug it up with a hammer and nail.
And you can't plug it up with paint from a pail.
And you can't plug it up with a big rubber plug.
And you can't make it better with a kiss and a hug.
But if the trees in the rainforest keep on making air,
And we all make sure that those trees stay right there,
Then maybe the air that the trees always make,
Can rise in the sky and fix up our mistake.
I'm planting my own tree, that's the least I can do
'Cause there's a hole in the sky where the rays come through.

# THE QUEEN OF OLD LOBSTERVILLE
## (HER MAJESTY OF MARTHA'S VINEYARD)

All hail the Queen of Old Lobsterville
With her royal blue shovel.
And pink pail to fill
With sea shells and hermit crabs,
Rare jewels of the ocean -
In her flip-flops and goggles and suntanning lotion.
If the waves are too choppy, she makes them be still -
And they will, for the Queen of good Old Lobsterville.
She can charm all the bluefish right out of the water!
She can dance with the mermaids like King Neptune's daughter!
All the boats bow their boughs to the Queen of the seas,
And the waves wave to her and they tickle her knees!
She's the worlds greatest grand castle sand engineer,
With her watering can and her sand castle gear.
She builds royal sand castles that reach for the sky,
With windows of sea glass and walls three feet high -
Then the tides tiptoe in on the wings of the wind
And washes away where castles had been.
But the tides bring the shells
And good skipping stone stones,
For the royal collection her majesty owns.
And when her pink pail is quite twice nicely filled,
Off walks the Queen of Old Lobsterville.
And the bluefish sing blues songs,
And terns whistle tunes -
As the Queen in her flip-flops fades over the dunes.
But her mermaids in waiting will wait in the sea
Till tomorrow's appointment with her majesty.
When she'll come once again with her pink pail to fill
They will wait for their Queen out in Old Lobsterville.

# GRANDPA'S A CHRISTMAS TREE

Grandpa shouted, "Look at me!
I'm a walking Christmas tree!"
He had taped a star on the top of his head.
On his nose and his ears he had glass balls of red.
And wrapped himself in some blinking light strings,
And grandmother said, "Well, of all the dumb things!
Why would you wear 'round your neck such a wreath?
And why dance with icicles stuck in your teeth?"
"Because, hon," said Grandpa, "because, darling dear . . .
Christmas time only comes round once a year!
And it makes me feel grand though I look rather funny.
But wait until Easter!  I'm gonna dress like a bunny."

# MY HEART'S A PAPER AIRPLANE

My heart's a paper airplane,
   Got a paper airplane for a heart.
Don't need no big propeller,
   Just a breeze to get my start.
Just a breeze will get me up there,
   Feeling good and light and free . . .
But, it's just a paper airplane . . .
   So, don't get rough with me.
'Cause if the pointy end gets beat on,
   Then my heart don't fly so well.
And if you go and step on it . . .
   Can I fix it?  I can't tell.
I'll try to mend it, open it up,
   And straighten it out and then . . .
Wait for the very next breeze of love
   To send it high again.

## DEAR SANTA GIVES A
## HUG TO THE WORLD

Dear Santa Claus gives a hug to the world,
To every boy and every girl.
His arms are long and strong and wide,
And warm to tuck us all inside.
To hold us close and safe from harm,
He holds the world in his gentle arms.
With love in his heart for every boy and every girl,
Dear Santa Claus gives a hug to the world.

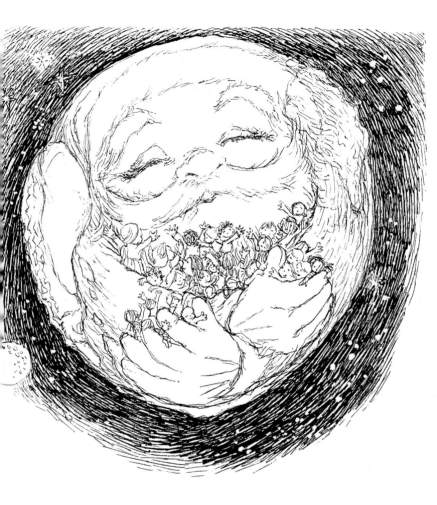

## SPIDERS

Do spiders play soccer?
If they don't, then they should.
With EIGHT legs to kick with
They'd be pretty good!

# PLAYING FOOTBALL
# WITH SAM

Hey!
Look at me!
Pass the ball over here!
I can outrun the defense
And get in the clear!
I can run for a touchdown!
I can run for it all!
Oh, Great!
Sam, my dog,
Intercepted the ball!

# MY PRAYER

Now I lay me down to sleep.
  I pray these promises I can keep.
To try to be gooder
  than I was today.
To not be so bossy
  when my friends and me play.
To try not to talk
  when my mouth's full of food.
To not pick my nose,
  'cause Mom says that that's rude.
To do all my chores
  without making a stink.
To try to like school
  where they tell me to think.
To remember to wash
  after playing in dirt.
And don't wipe my hands
  on my pants or my shirt.
These are things to remember.
  So, Dear Lord, I pray. . .
That I remember them tomorrow
  'cause I forgot them today.
                Amen.

# MELINDA'S CATAMARAN

Melinda's pet monster,
The Catamaran, swallowed a
33 piece marching band.
Not the musicians, mind you.
No ladies and gents. . .
But the Catamaran
Gobbled the instruments.
Melinda said,
"Cat. . . Did you gobble the drum?"
Cat opened his mouth. . .
And went Rump Tee Tum Tum.
"Did you gobble the clarinet, trumpet and oboe?"
Cat opened his mouth. . .
And each horn played a solo.
"Did you eat all the saxophones, tubas and flutes?"
From her pet monster's mouth. . .
Came some Root a Toot Toots.
"Tell me," said Melinda,
"How'd you finish your meal?"
Her Catamaran burped the glockenspiel.
Ever since then, when her monster says "Hi,"
It's like a parade on the Fourth of July.

# ODE TO 3 GUYS YOU DON'T WANT
# TO HAVE AT YOUR PARTY

Toe-tapping Willie
And Sigfreid and Jake
Live to dance
On your Birthday Cake.
They'll ride on a dragon
From their home outside Boston,
And come to your party
Just to dance on your frostin'!
They don't have to know you,
They'll just find out, and come!
They'll hear its your Birthday
And come on the run!
They'll dance on your icing!
"The Twist" and "The Fly"!
And don't try to stop them!
No!  Don't even try!
Till they "Boogaloo," "Hucklebuck,"
"Cool-Jerk," and "Shake". . .
Toe-tapping Willie and
Sigfreid and Jake.

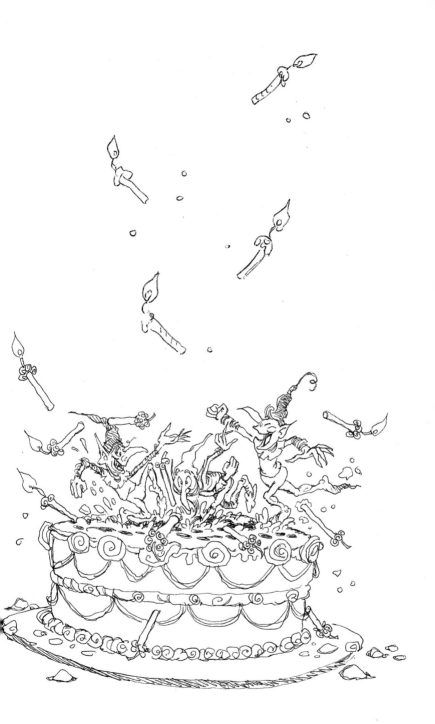

## IF I WERE A PIRATE

If I were a pirate
With a Spanish galleon
And a crew of cut-throats
Who'd do what I say,
I would drop my anchor
In Pennsylvania
And steal all the chocolate bars
In Hershey, PA!

# THE LIVING ROOM DANCE

Turn up the radio! LOUD!
Take a chance!
Do the "All-alone-in-the-
Living-room-dance!"
Do the Locomotion!
The Swim and the Twist!
Do the Funky Chicken!
Shake it like this!
Dance on the sofa!
Do the Bop and the Slop!
Do the "Up-on-the-coffee-
table-hip-bunny-hop!"
Dance around in your t-shirt!
Do it in your socks!
All alone in the living room, baby,
EVERYBODY ROCKS!

# SWAMPWATER JACK

Way down in the bayou, down in the swamp
Where the gators are big with teeth that chomp
And waters too black for the fishes to swim,
That's where he lives. Don't go looking for him.
That's where he lives, name is Swampwater Jack.
If you're looking for him, well you better turn back.
Many have tried to find his gold. . .
That pirate gold that Old Swampwater stoled
From the wicked Pirate Captain Dan
Down off the coast of Louisianne.
He took all the gold, every shillin' and pence
And Old Swampwater Jack ain't been heard of since.
But he stuck up a sign in the Black Bayou
Says, "I'd turn back, if I were you."
And he moved way way back
Where the swamp water bubbles,
And boils with gators just looking for trouble. . .
There he sits with his gold and remembers his deed. . .
But Old Jack forgot that old Pirates can't read. . .
Especially wicked old Pirates turned ghosts. . .
Who come for revenge from the Louisianne coast.
Was it Captain Dan's ghost and the ghosts of his crew?
Was it, Swampwater Jack? Were they coming for you?
I'm not gonna tell, 'cause I don't really know. . .
And ghosts aren't supposed to be real,
Don't you know. . .
So the gators that smile must surely be wrong. . .
It's just, no one's seen Jack in so very long. . .
But he used to live back where mean gators swim. . .
And no one I know's goin' lookin' for him.

# BILLY AND THE SNOWBALL

Billy made a snowball
And he put it in the freezer.
Billy made a snowball
For his sister just to tease her.
I'll take it out in summertime.
I'll hit her in the head.
I'll slush it down her pajama top
When she's sleeping in the bed.
Billy's sister made a snowball, too.
She was thinking a similar thing.
But his sister threw her snowball
And hit Billy in the Spring.

## DREAMS

Does anyone know ---
      Where the dreams go?
The dreams that somebody forgot?
Does anyone know ---
      Where the dreams go?
All the dreams that someone never got?
They must be out there somewhere,
Forgotten dreams in the wind.
Are they waiting for someone to reach out
To remember and dream them again?

# THE INCREDIBLE CREATURE BAND

I met a golden unicorn
And asked her if she'd play her horn.
I met a Snarf from outer space
Who played a real mean stand up bass.
I met a couple cockatoos
Who really wailed and sang the blues.
Down in the swamp I met a croc
Who rocked and rocked around the clock.
I met a dog who had no bone
Instead he had a slide trombone.
I met a couple real hip yaks.
Funky yaks that played the sax.
Now we all travel all over the land ---
We are. . .
      "THE
           INCREDIBLE
              CREATURE
                BAND."

# A LITTLE FAVOR FOR THE NORTH WIND

If you're ever in New England
And it's down around the fall
And if you have a moment
Any freebie time at all. . .
Would you do a little favor
For The North Wind if you please?
He'd appreciate it muchly
If you'd look up in the trees---
And if you happen to see an elf
or elves up on the branch,
If they're sleeping holding paint brushes
By any little chance . . .
Would you wake the little loafers up,
And tell them to roll up their sleeves?!
And tell them to get back to work!
They're supposed to be painting the leaves!

# PLEASE DON'T WAKE THE DRAGON

Please don't talk.
Don't make a peep.
You might wake the dragon.
The dragon's asleep.
Please don't let
Your tongue start waggin'.
Don't make a sound now.
You might wake the dragon.
Son't say a word now.
You better not talk.
And you might try and
Tiptoe your quietest walk!
And pretend you're not nervous!
He might hear you shake!
Be QUIET, I said!
Oops!
Too late!
He's AWAKE!

# I'M GREAT!

I'm great!  I'm marvelous!
I'm terrific!  Yessiree!
I'm the very best there is
At the job of being ME!
Just ask anybody!
Anybody that I know!
They'll tell you I'm the very best!
The best ME that they know!
I look like ME!  I laugh like ME!
I even talk like ME!
I run like ME!  Have fun like ME,
I even walk like ME!
I'm incredible!  Fantastic!
I'm FAN-TAB-ULOUS, it's true!
I'm the best me I can be,
And you're the best YOU, too!

# I WANT TO RENT AN ELEPHANT

I want to rent an elephant
So I can ride to school.
I want to rent an elephant
So I can look real cool.
I'll feed him high-test peanuts
So he'll go really fast!
And all the kids will be amazed
As we go roaring past.
So give him a saddle, silver trimmed . . .
With racing stripes of red . . .
And a helmet like a race car driver
With goggles for his head.
Then find me a pair of sneakers, No . . .
You better make that two!
TWO pair of elephant sneakers,
Make 'em size 7 hundred and two.
So quick!  Rent me an elephant!
I've always wanted to try one!
And if I like the elephant . . .
Who knows?  I just might buy one!

WE'RE #1!

## KITE

I started flying this kite 'bout an hour ago.
What I'm not really sure of, you see . . .
Is when exactly I stopped flying my kite
And my kite started flying me?

# DANDELION

I wished upon a dandelion.
I wished a wish today.
I wished upon a dandelion,
And then it blew away.
The dandelion flittered
Into pieces all over the yard.
I wished upon a dandelion, but . . .
I must have wished too hard.

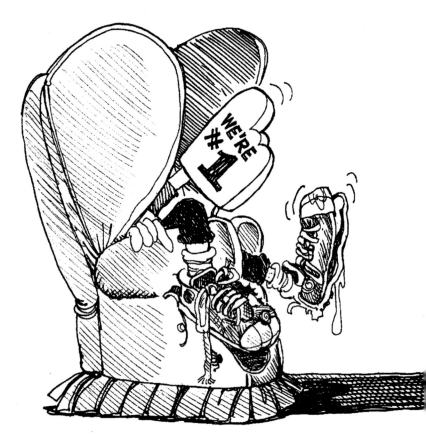

# DIRTY SNEAKERS

Who has the dirtiest sneakers?
I DO!  I DO!  I DO!
Are they brown and black and crusty?
YES, THEY ARE!
And smelly too!
They're grimey and gritty,
And holey and pitty,
And greasy and grungy,
And mossy and mungy,
And they smell like SKUNKS,
And TURPENTINE!
These horrible,
BEAUTIFUL sneakers of mine!

## JUMPIN'

When it comes to jumpin'
Jump so high I can't be beat.
Don't need no fancy sneakers,
'Cause I got rubber feet.

## SKY DANCER

Sky dancer, that's what I want to be.
Sky dancer, it's got to feel so free. . .
To glide along the moon and Mars,
Leap in the wind and touch the stars.
Sky dancer, that's what I want to be.

# TWO INCHES HIGH MCBLY

Once upon a time in the forest of Sly
Lived a man named McBly who stood two inches high
McBly was so short that a whole day would pass
Before he could climb up one small blade of grass.
So he figured a way to move fast through the thicket.
He'd ride on the back of a fast hopping cricket.
McBly built a boat out of one single twig
(You can sail on a twig if you aren't very big.)
And McBly as you know was just two inches high.
So the twig was like a scooner to Mr. McBly
Between sailing & hopping he got along well
Back & forth to his castle made out of a shell.
With turrets of mushrooms, some moss for a rug
And blankets of leaves, he was warm safe and snug.
The only problem, it seemed, for little McBly
Was when a bear or wolf or a fox ran on by.
When you're two inches high, then the littlest shake
Like an animals footsteps are like an earthquake.
And he was sometimes mistaken by a cat for a mouse
So he'd have to hide out in his shell of a house
But said McBly, "All my troubles are small.
And they should be, cause I'm only two inches tall"
Then he hopped upon a postage stamp
and glided through the sky
Free and easygoing, Two-inch high McBly.

# MY RECORDS

A record can be a friend, a mood,
  A feeling or a memory.
    I've got a lot of records myself,
      And they're all those things to me.
I keep all my records, the old and new,
  In an old black metal rack.
    My favorites are right up here in front.
      My second favorites just toward the back.
When I wake up in the morning,
  I put on the happy ones.
    Songs of cheerful mornings,
      Fresh cut grass and shining Suns.
And when I have to make my bed,
  Fix the pillows, and straighten the sheets,
    Then I rock around the bedposts,
      To the ones with the bopping beats.

When I come home from a day of school,
   And its been a crummy day,
      I put on the songs of heartbreak,
         'Cause the blues are good that way.
It's nice to hear a tear or two,
   A slow song sung real blue,
      When you're just a little blue yourself,
         Sad songs can see you through.
And when I'm ready to go to sleep,
   I put on a real big stack.
      A pile of my records
         that keep playing back to back.
I set it so the tone arm
   keeps repeating that last song,
      And I fall asleep
         with those words spinning 'round,
And the band plays
   on
      and
         on . . . .

# IT'S ME AGAIN

Hey, God . . . It's me again. . .
Just simple little me.
I want to thank you for making today so good
And for making my best climbing tree.
And thank you for the whippoorwill
I heard outside my window -
That one I heard about 7:00.
That's a nice way to wake up, you know.
And thanks a lot for the way clothes smell
When Mom dries them outside on the clothesline.
And thank you for my favorite chair.
And thank you for the sunshine.
And thank you for going fishing.
And thank you for my very best friend,
And thank you for my dog Sandy, God.
OOPS,
   I almost
     forgot . . . .
       Amen.

# CLOUDS

Heather Peacher asked about the weather.
"How do clouds stick together?
How come clouds, day after day . . .
Don't break into pieces and flitter away?
Do the clouds come stuck together
With some kind of goo?
Does God glue them up
With God's own secret glue?
What is the answer?" asked Heather Peacher.
"It's time for recess," said the teacher.

# I DON'T KNOW HOW

I don't know how to sail a boat.
I don't know how to sail.
I want to learn, but golly gee,
What if I try and fail.
I don't know how to ride a horse.
I don't know how to ride.
I want to learn, but if I fall,
Where will I run and hide?
I don't know how to swim and dive.
I don't know how to swim.
I want to learn but what if I can't
I better not jump in.
Hey, somebody pushed me!
Hey! They pushed me in the pool!
Hey! I WASN'T READY!
Hey! It's kind of nice and cool!
And look at me, I'm swimming!
Hey, now I'm having fun!
Thanks for giving me the push . . .
I guess I needed one.

## I'M A SECRET AGENT

On my secret bicycle
I ride the secret road
I've got my secret orders
Written in secret code
To find the secret keys
That will unlock the secret locks
So I can get a cookie
From your secret cookie box

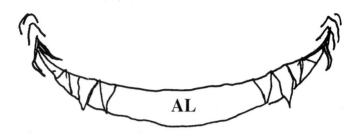

**AL**

Have you heard about Al Crocodile?
He's got a smile as long as a mile.
He licks his chops
  When a boater stops---
    'Cause Al hasn't ate in a while.

## EVERYTHING I KNOW ABOUT ART

Think of an IT.
Think of a SO.
Think of a WHAT'S IT CALLED.
Think it and go!
Grab a pencil!  Grab a pen!
Draw what you thought of. . .
Then do it again.

## RUNAWAY SHADOW

Has anybody seen my shadow?
   I think it ran away.
I haven't seen that shadow,
   Since the day before yesterday.
We used to do everything together.
   We were close as two buddies could be.
I was really attached to my shadow...
   And I thought he was attached to me.

# TICKLY GRASS

I'd rather have tickly grass
under my feet,
Than a city-walkin' sidewalk
of hard ol' concrete.
Even if I got bugs, worms,
and salamanders
between ALL my toes
('cause out in the tickly grass
*ANYTHING* goes).
I'd rather not walk on that
scratchy concrete.
Nope.
Give me some tickly grass under my feet.

# WHAT BOTHERS FRANKENSTEIN?

Frankenstein
Doesn't mind . . .
Nails in his neck,
Screws in his toes,
Rain on his brain,
Or ill-fitting clothes,
Big iron shoes,
Socks full of muck,
A zipper in his neck
That always gets stuck,
Stitches, staples,
Grease and glue,
Skin that's
Greenish-grayish-blue.
But there is one thing
That bugs him.
One thing that never fails . . .
Scratching the blackboard
With your fingernails!!

# KISS TODAY GOODMORNING

Kiss today goodmorning
When the sky pops up today.
Give the sky a smile first,
Before you're on your way.
Kiss today goodmorning.
Look at the big fat world around you.
Birds are singing for you.
Little miracles surround you.
Like that pocketful of sunlight,
That through clouds still shines through.
Put that sunlight in your pocket
'Cause today belongs to you.

Dear Santa Claus,
My name is Johnny.
I've been naughty and mean.
I don't eat my meals
and I snack in between.
I don't make my bed.
I don't fold my clothes.
I don't brush my teeth right
and I pick my nose.
I won't take a bath.
I never shampoo.
And I never, ever, ever,
close my mouth when I chew.
And I throw out my socks
when I've worn them too long.
On math tests I get
at least twelve answers wrong.
But if you bring me a present
this year like you SHOULD . . .
I promise NEXT year
I will try to be good.

# THE WIND

The Wind can whistle.
The Wind can moan.
Some call the Wind "Mariah."
The Wind can rustle the leaves so much
That, Man!  They scoot right by ya!
The Wind can howl.
The Wind can sing.
It can blow the poor trees bare.
But. . . the one thing it *can't* do
Is just be STILL. . .
'Cause then, it ain't WIND, it's AIR.

# THE RAINBOW MAN

This is a story about the Rainbow Man.
A wizard unlike any other.
To the ancient stars he was a child.
To the Earth, he was a brother.
Once upon a magic time,
In a land not far from here,
Where the grass is always soft and green
And the brook runs crystal clear.
Where the song the birds are singing
Joins the whistle of the breeze.
Where the frogs all play their banjoes
To the faces in the trees. . .
There lived a bearded wizard
Who was loved throughout the land.
A gentle, quiet wizard
Who they called the Rainbow Man.
You might not have known he was a wizard
Just to stop and look at him.
'Cause he didn't have a wizard's hat
With stars across the brim.
And he didn't have any magic wands,
Or charms, or magic lockets.
No card tricks hidden up his sleeves
Or twinkles in his pockets.
But the Rainbow Man had a magic *heart*
That could glow with such a glow
It would shine upon the forest folk
And make their *own* hearts grow.
And the Rainbow Man had magic eyes
That could see the dreams inside you. . .

And he could turn your dreams
Into things so real
That they stood right there beside you.
"Just look within yourself," he'd say,
"For that dream you hold most dear.
Look, and search, and see that dream
Till it's bright, and real, and clear.
Then take that dream wherever you go,
And see it everyday.
And hold it in your heart and mind,"
The Rainbow Man would say.
"You *all* have the magic.
You *all* have the *heart* to make
All your wishes come true!
This is the gift I was given,
And the gift that I now give to you."
So, the caterpillar dreamed
Of sprouting wings
And fluttering free through the sky.
And he dreamed, and he wished
Until one perfect day . . .
He became a butterfly.
The newborn fowl out in the field
Dreamed of being a gold unicorn
And she grew up so wise,
And so loving, and free,
You'd swear that she *did* grow that horn.
And that reindeer
That carried his dream everyday
In a spot in the front of his head
About spreading joy throughout the world,
Found himself pulling Santa's own sled.
Yes, The Rainbow Man was a wizard
And though he moved on a while ago . . .
His magic still lives on and on
And his gift just seems to grow.

# IMAGINE A BIRD

(This poem works really well if you can close your
eyes and have someone read it to you, too)

Imagine a bird.
A bird colored white.
A bird colored white
Like the brightest of lights,
Like every glimmer and shine
All rolled into one.
A bird colored white
Soars into the sun.
And round through it's shimmering
White golden rays,
That can golden up even
The grayest of days ---
Then down soars the bird
All glowing and free ---
Down through the sky
Then it pierces the sea.
Down through the spray
And into the foam.
It swims through the sea
As if it were home.
Then UP, UP again
To the cool sky of blue.
This bird can go anywhere
And this bird is YOU.

# MONKEY HOUSE

Welcome to the Monkey House!
The Monkey House!  The Monkey House!
Welcome to the Monkey House!
Come in!  Come in!  Come in!
Have you met the marmosets,
Orangutans, and chimpanzees?
Have you met the gorilla twins?
Come in!  Come in!  Come in!
Did you bring a banana bunch?
Banana bunch?  Banana bunch?
You *didn't* bring my monkeys lunch?!
Get out!  Get out!  Get out!

# NIGHT LIGHTS & PILLOW FIGHTS

Take a bath and get a hug,
Toys and clothes left on the rug.
Fresh, clean sheets that smell so fine
From drying outside on the line.
Pajamas with feet with one toe showing,
Pillow fights and night lights glowing.
A book to read, a rhyme or two.
A kiss good-night. An "I Love You."
Now get to sleep, you sleepy head,
And no more jumping on the bed!

# STRAWBERRY RHUBARB LOVE SONG

Strawberry Rhubarb!
Sweet Potato Pie!
You're the apple sauce
Of my eye.
Jest as spicy!
Jest as sweet!
I love ya as much as
I love to eat!